Flutter for App Development with Dart

A Comprehensive Guide

Benjamin Evans

2

Copyright © 2024 Benjamin Evans

DEDICATION

To the relentless seekers of knowledge, the curious minds tirelessly decoding the mysteries of algorithms and code. This book is dedicated to you, the coders who embrace the challenges of neural networks with fervor and determination. May these pages serve as stepping stones on your journey, empowering you to unravel the complexities of this dynamic field and craft solutions that shape the future. Your passion fuels the innovation that drives our world forward, and for that, I extend my deepest gratitude and admiration.

CONTENTS

ACKNOWLEDGMENTS

I would like to extend my sincere gratitude to all those who have contributed to the realization of this book. First and foremost, I am indebted to my family for their unwavering support and encouragement throughout this endeavor. Their love and understanding have been my anchor in the stormy seas of writing.

I am deeply thankful to the experts whose guidance and insights have illuminated my path and enriched the content of this book. Their mentorship has been invaluable in shaping my understanding and refining my ideas.

I also extend my appreciation to those whose constructive feedback and insightful suggestions have helped polish this work to its finest form.

Furthermore, I am grateful to the countless individuals whose research, publications, and contributions have paved the way for the insights shared in these pages.

Last but not least, I express my heartfelt appreciation to the readers who embark on this journey with me. Your curiosity and engagement breathe life into these words, and it is for you that this book exists.

Thank you all for being part of this remarkable journey.

CHAPTER 1

INTRODUCTION TO FLUTTER AND DART

Welcome to the exciting world of mobile app development with Flutter! This chapter will lay the groundwork for your journey by introducing you to Flutter, the framework you'll be using, and Dart, the language that powers it. We'll also explore the benefits of using Flutter and guide you through setting up your development environment. Finally, we'll create a simple "Hello World" app to get your hands dirty with the basics.

1.1 What is Flutter?

Imagine building beautiful and performant mobile applications for both Android and iOS using a single codebase. That's the magic of Flutter! Developed by Google, Flutter is a free and open-source framework that allows you to create native-looking apps for various platforms, including:

- Mobile (Android & iOS)
- Web
- Desktop (Windows, macOS, Linux)
- Embedded devices

Benefits of using Flutter:

- **Fast Development:** Flutter utilizes a technique called "hot reload," which allows you to see changes reflected in your app almost instantly as you code. This significantly speeds up the development process, letting you experiment and iterate quickly.
- **Expressive UI:** Flutter offers a rich set of widgets for building visually stunning and customizable user interfaces. Unlike traditional hybrid app development, Flutter renders UI elements directly on the device, resulting in a smooth and native feel.
- **Single Codebase:** With Flutter, you write your app's core logic in Dart, a single programming language. This eliminates the need to learn and maintain separate codebases for different platforms, saving you time and resources.

- **Large Community:** Flutter boasts a vibrant and active developer community. You'll find plenty of resources, tutorials, and support available online if you ever get stuck.

1.2 Understanding Dart

Dart is a general-purpose, object-oriented programming language specifically designed for building modern web and mobile applications. Here's what makes it a perfect fit for Flutter development:

- **Type Safety:** Dart is a statically typed language, which means the data type of a variable is known at compile time. This helps catch potential errors early in the development process, leading to more robust and stable apps.
- **Null Safety:** Dart enforces null safety, ensuring variables are either assigned a value or explicitly marked as nullable. This prevents null pointer exceptions, a common source of crashes in other languages.

- **Modern Features:** Dart offers several modern features such as garbage collection, asynchronous programming, and closures, which make writing clean and maintainable code easier.

- **Learning Curve:** If you're familiar with languages like Java, JavaScript, or C++, picking up Dart shouldn't be too challenging. Its syntax is relatively easy to learn, and there are plenty of resources available to help you get started.

1.3 Setting Up Your Development Environment

Now that you're excited about Flutter and Dart, let's get your development environment ready! Here's what you'll need:

- **Flutter SDK:** Download and install the Flutter SDK from the official website (https://docs.flutter.dev/get-started/install). It comes bundled with the Dart SDK.

- **IDE:** Choose your preferred Integrated Development Environment (IDE) for coding. Popular options for

Flutter development include:

- ○ **Android Studio:** A powerful IDE by Google with built-in support for Flutter development.
- ○ **Visual Studio Code:** A lightweight and versatile code editor with Flutter plugins that provide excellent support.
- ○ **IntelliJ IDEA:** A full-featured IDE by JetBrains with Flutter plugins for advanced development needs.

Each IDE has its own installation and configuration process. Refer to the official documentation of your chosen IDE for detailed instructions on setting up Flutter support.

1.4 Creating Your First Flutter App

Let's create a simple "Hello World" app to get comfortable with the basic structure of a Flutter project. Here's a step-by-step guide:

1. **Open your IDE.**
2. **Create a new Flutter project.** Each IDE has its own

way of creating a new project. Refer to the documentation for specific instructions.

3. **Navigate to the main application file.** In most cases, this will be a file named main.dart.

Here's a breakdown of the code you'll find in the main.dart file:

```dart
import 'package:flutter/material.dart';

void main() {
  runApp(MyApp());
}

class MyApp extends StatelessWidget {
  @override
  Widget build(BuildContext context) {
    return MaterialApp(
      home: Scaffold(
        appBar: AppBar(
          title: Text('Hello World!'),
        ),
```

```
    body: Center(
      child: Text('Welcome to Flutter!'),
      ),
     ),
    );
  }
}
```

Let's break down the code in main.dart to understand how it builds our "Hello World" app:

1. import 'package:flutter/material.dart';: This line imports the material.dart package, which provides essential widgets for building user interfaces in Flutter.

2. void main() { ... }: This is the main entry point of your application. The code inside the main function is executed when the app starts.

3. runApp(MyApp());: This line calls the runApp

function from the material.dart package. It takes a Widget as an argument, which is the root widget of your app's UI hierarchy. In this case, we're passing an instance of our MyApp class.

4. class MyApp extends StatelessWidget { ... }: This defines a class named MyApp that extends the StatelessWidget class. Stateless widgets are used for UI elements that don't change dynamically.

5. @override and Widget build(BuildContext context) { ... }: The @override annotation signifies that we're overriding the build method inherited from the StatelessWidget class. This method is responsible for building the widget's UI and returning a Widget that represents the UI structure. The BuildContext argument provides information about the widget's location in the widget tree.

6. return MaterialApp(...);: This line returns a MaterialApp widget, which is the foundation for

most Flutter apps built with Material Design principles. It provides features like app title, navigation, and theming.

7. home: Scaffold(...);: The home property of MaterialApp specifies the widget that will be displayed as the app's home screen. Here, we're using the Scaffold widget, which provides a basic layout structure with an app bar and a body area for content.

8. appBar: AppBar(...);: The appBar property of Scaffold defines the app bar widget displayed at the top of the screen. Here, we're using the AppBar widget with a title property set to "Hello World!".

9. body: Center(...);: The body property of Scaffold defines the content displayed in the main area of the screen. We're using the Center widget to center our content horizontally and vertically.

10. child: Text('Welcome to Flutter!');: Finally, the Center widget's child property holds a Text widget that displays the message "Welcome to Flutter!".

Running Your First Flutter App

1. **Save the changes** to your main.dart file.
2. **Run the app** using your IDE's built-in functionality. This will typically involve a "Run" or "Debug" button or menu option.

Once you run the app, you should see a new window or emulator appear with the title "Hello World!" displayed in the app bar and the message "Welcome to Flutter!" centered on the screen. Congratulations, you've successfully created your first Flutter app!

This chapter provided a high-level introduction to Flutter and Dart. You learned about the benefits of using Flutter, the key features of Dart, and how to set up your development environment. Finally, you created a simple

"Hello World" app to get a taste of the basic structure and workflow in Flutter development.

As you progress through this book, you'll delve deeper into building more complex and interactive Flutter applications, exploring various widgets, functionalities, and design patterns.

CHAPTER 2

DART PROGRAMMING FUNDAMENTALS

Dart, the language powering Flutter, is the foundation for building your applications. This chapter dives into the core concepts of Dart programming, equipping you with the essential tools to write clean, efficient, and maintainable code.

2.1 Variables, Data Types, and Operators

Data manipulation and organization are crucial aspects of programming. In Dart, variables act as containers that store data of specific types.

- **Declaring and Initializing Variables:**

  You declare a variable using the var keyword followed by the variable name and optionally a type annotation. Here's an example:

```
var name = "John Doe"; // String type, inferred by Dart
int age = 30;
double pi = 3.14159; // Double type for floating-point
numbers
bool isStudent = true;
```

- Dart allows type inference, meaning it can automatically determine the data type based on the assigned value in some cases. However, explicitly specifying types can enhance code readability and maintainability.

- **Understanding Data Types:**

  Dart offers various data types to represent different kinds of information:

  - **int:** Represents whole numbers (e.g., 10, -5).
  - **double:** Represents floating-point numbers with decimals (e.g., 3.14, -12.5).
  - **String:** Represents textual data enclosed in

quotes (e.g., "Hello, world!").

- ○ **bool:** Represents Boolean values, either true or false.
- ○ **List:** An ordered collection of items, can hold elements of different types (e.g., [1, 2.5, "apple"]).
- ○ **Map:** An unordered collection of key-value pairs (e.g., {"name": "Alice", "age": 25}).
- ○ **Set:** An unordered collection of unique items (e.g., {1, 2, 2} will only contain 1 and 2).
- Choosing the appropriate data type ensures your variables hold the intended kind of data, preventing potential errors.

- **Performing Operations with Operators:**

Operators allow you to manipulate and compare data stored in variables. Dart provides various operators for arithmetic, comparison, and logical operations:

| Operator | Description | Example | |---|---|---| | +, -, *, / | Arithmetic operations for addition, subtraction, multiplication, and division | x + y, a - b, c * d, e / f | | % | Modulo operator, returns the remainder of a division | 10 % 3 (result: 1) | | ==, !=, <, >, <=, >= | Comparison operators for equality, inequality, and ordering | x == y, a != b, c < d, e >= f | | &&, ||, ! | Logical operators for AND, OR, and NOT | x > 0 && y < 10, a == true || b == false, !isWorking |

2.2 Control Flow Statements

Programs don't always execute linearly. Control flow statements determine the order in which code blocks run based on certain conditions.

- **Making Decisions with if/else statements:**

  Use if statements to execute code if a condition is true. Optionally, you can add else blocks for alternative behavior when the condition is false.

```dart
int age = 20;
if (age >= 18) {
  print("You are eligible to vote.");
} else {
  print("You are not eligible to vote.");
}
```

- Nested if statements allow for more complex decision-making logic.

- **Looping through Data using for and while loops:**

  Loops allow you to repeat a block of code multiple times.

  - for **loops:** Useful for iterating through a known number of times or elements in a collection.

```
List<String> fruits = ["apple", "banana", "orange"];
for (String fruit in fruits) {
 print(fruit);

}
```

- o while **loops:** Execute a code block as long as a condition remains true.

```
int count = 0;
while (count < 5) {
 print("Count: $count");
 count++;

}
```

- **Utilizing switch statements for multi-way branching:**

switch statements provide a more concise way to handle multiple conditions compared to nested if statements.

```
String grade = "A";

switch (grade) {

  case "A":

    print("Excellent!");

    break;

  case "B":

    print("Very good!");

    break;

  case "C":

    print("Good.");

    break;

  default:

    print("Invalid grade.");

}
```

2.3 Functions and Methods

Functions are reusable blocks of code that perform specific

tasks. They promote code modularity and organization.

- **Defining and Calling Functions:**

    You define a function using the def keyword (not present in Dart) followed by the function name, parentheses for parameters, an optional return type, and the function body enclosed in curly braces ({}). Here's the equivalent structure in Dart:

```dart
String greet(String name) {
  return "Hello, $name!";
}



String message = greet("Alice");
print(message); // Output: Hello, Alice!
```

In this example, the greet function takes a name parameter (string type) and returns a greeting message. The print function is used to display the returned value.

- **Passing Arguments and Returning Values:**

  Functions can accept arguments (inputs) and optionally return values (outputs). Arguments provide data to the function, while return values allow functions to send data back to the calling code.

- **Understanding the Concept of Methods in Classes:**

  Functions defined within a class are called methods. They have access to the class's properties and can operate on its data. Methods are essential for object-oriented programming, which we'll explore next.

2.4 Object-Oriented Programming (OOP) in Dart

Object-oriented programming (OOP) is a paradigm for structuring code around objects. Objects encapsulate data (properties) and behavior (methods), promoting modularity, reusability, and maintainability.

- **Creating Classes and Objects:**

    A class is a blueprint that defines the properties and methods of objects. You create objects (instances) from a class.

```dart
class Person {
  String name;
  int age;

  void speak() {
    print("Hello, my name is $name!");
  }
}
```

```
Person john = Person(); // Create an object named john

john.name = "John Doe";

john.age = 30;

john.speak(); // Output: Hello, my name is John Doe!
```

In this example, the Person class defines properties (name and age) and a method (speak). We create an object john of type Person and access its properties and methods.

- **Inheritance, Polymorphism, and Encapsulation:**

   OOP concepts like inheritance, polymorphism, and encapsulation further enhance code organization and reusability.

   - **Inheritance:** Allows creating new classes (subclasses) that inherit properties and methods from existing classes (superclasses). Subclasses can also add their own functionalities.

- o **Polymorphism:** Enables objects of different classes to respond to the same method call in different ways, promoting flexibility.
- o **Encapsulation:** Bundles data (properties) and methods within a class, restricting direct access to properties and controlling data manipulation through methods.

By mastering these core concepts of Dart programming fundamentals, you'll have a solid foundation for building effective and maintainable Flutter applications. The following chapters will delve deeper into specific aspects of Flutter development, utilizing the knowledge gained here.

CHAPTER 3

WORKING WITH WIDGETS IN FLUTTER

The user interface (UI) is the face of your app, and in Flutter, you build UIs using widgets. This chapter dives into the world of widgets, the fundamental building blocks of Flutter applications.

3.1 Understanding the Widget Tree

Imagine your app's UI as a tree structure. The root of this tree is a special widget called MaterialApp (for Material Design apps) or WidgetsApp (for general purpose apps). Every other widget in your app branches out from this root, forming a hierarchy that defines the layout and visual elements. Each widget is responsible for a specific part of the UI, and its properties determine how it appears and behaves.

There are two main types of widgets in Flutter:

- **Stateless Widgets:** These widgets represent UI elements that are fixed and don't change dynamically based on user interaction or data. They are simple and efficient for static UI elements.

- **Stateful Widgets:** Stateful widgets are used for UI elements that can change their appearance or behavior based on user input, data updates, or other events. They maintain internal state information that can be modified.

3.2 Basic Widgets for Layouts

Flutter provides a rich set of widgets to organize and structure your app's layout. Here are some fundamental layout widgets:

- **Container:** A versatile widget that acts as a container for other widgets. You can customize its padding, margin, color, and other visual properties.

Container(
  child: Text('Hello, world!'),

padding: EdgeInsets.all(16.0), // Add padding around the text

color: Colors.blue[100], // Set a light blue background color

)

- **Row:** Arranges widgets horizontally in a row, similar to a table row.

```
Row(
  children: [
    Text('Name: '),
    Text('John Doe'),
  ],
)
```

- **Column:** Arranges widgets vertically in a column, similar to a table column.

```
Column(
  children: [
    Text('Title: '),
    Text('Software Engineer'),
  ],
```

)

- **Stack:** Overlaps widgets on top of each other. Useful for creating layered layouts or implementing z-axis effects.

```
Stack(
  children: [
    Container(
      color: Colors.red,
      width: 100,
      height: 100,
    ),
    Center(
      child: Text('I am on top!'),
    ),
  ],
)
```

By combining these basic layout widgets, you can create more complex and structured UIs for your app.

3.3 Text and Image Widgets

- **Text Widget:** Displays textual content on the screen. You can customize its style (font, size, color), alignment, and more using various properties.

```
Text(
  'This is a heading text.',
  style: TextStyle(
    fontSize: 20.0,
    fontWeight: FontWeight.bold,
  ),
)
```

- **Image Widget:** Displays images from assets or remote URLs.

```
Image.asset('assets/images/logo.png')   // Load image from assets folder
```

```
Image.network('https://example.com/image.jpg') // Load image from URL
```

Flutter provides features for image scaling, caching, and placeholder widgets to optimize image loading and performance.

3.4 Adding User Interaction with Buttons

Buttons are essential for user interaction in your app. Flutter offers various button types:

- **RaisedButton:** A standard raised button with a shadow effect.

```
RaisedButton(
  onPressed: () {
    print('Button clicked!');
  },
  child: Text('Click me'),
)
```

- The onPressed callback defines the action to be performed when the button is pressed.
- **FloatingActionButton:** A circular floating action button often used for primary actions.

```
FloatingActionButton(
  onPressed: () {
    print('Add new item');
  },
  child: Icon(Icons.add),
```

)

- **IconButton:** A button with an icon for concise actions.

```
IconButton(
  icon: Icon(Icons.delete),
  onPressed: () {
    print('Delete item');
  },
)
```

By incorporating these interactive elements, you make your app more engaging and responsive to user input.

CHAPTER 4

BUILDING STATEFUL WIDGETS AND STATE MANAGEMENT

While stateless widgets are great for static UI elements, Flutter's true power shines with stateful widgets. This chapter delves into stateful widgets, state management techniques, and how they work together to create dynamic and interactive UIs.

4.1 Stateful Widgets and the BuildContext

Stateful widgets are the workhorses of dynamic UIs. They maintain internal state information that can change over time, triggering UI updates to reflect those changes. Unlike stateless widgets, stateful widgets have a lifecycle that governs their creation, updates, and destruction.

Understanding the Life Cycle:

- **initState():** Called once when the widget is first created. Use this to perform any one-time initialization tasks, like fetching data from an API.

- **didChangeDependencies():** Called when the widget's dependencies change (e.g., parent widget updates).

- **build(BuildContext context):** Called whenever the widget's state changes or it needs to be rebuilt. This method returns a widget that represents the UI of the stateful widget.

- **didUpdateWidget(covariant MyWidget oldWidget):** Called when the widget receives new configuration data (e.g., props change).

- **deactivate():** Called when the widget is removed from the widget tree but still kept in memory.

- **dispose():** Called when the widget is permanently removed from the widget tree. Use this to clean up resources like listeners or subscriptions.

BuildContext:

The BuildContext argument passed to the build method provides contextual information about the widget's location in the widget tree. You can use it to access the state of the current widget and its ancestors, as well as perform various operations like navigation.

Code Example:

```
class Counter extends StatefulWidget {
  @override
  _CounterState createState() => _CounterState();
}

class _CounterState extends State<Counter> {
  int _count = 0;

  @override
  void initState() {
    super.initState();
    // One-time initialization (e.g., fetching data)
  }

  @override
  Widget build(BuildContext context) {
    return Center(
```

```dart
child: Column(
  mainAxisAlignment: MainAxisAlignment.center,
  children: [
    Text(
      'Count: $_count',
      style: TextStyle(fontSize: 24.0),
    ),
    Row(
      mainAxisAlignment: MainAxisAlignment.center,
      children: [
        ElevatedButton(
          onPressed: () => setState(() => _count++),
          child: Text('Increment'),
        ),
        SizedBox(width: 10.0),
        ElevatedButton(
          onPressed: () => setState(() => _count--),
          child: Text('Decrement'),
        ),
      ],
```

```
        ),
      ],
    ),
  );
}
}
```

In this example, the _count variable represents the state of the Counter widget. The setState method is used to update the state, which triggers the build method to be called again with the updated state, effectively rebuilding the UI with the new count value.

4.2 The setState() Method

The setState method is the heart of state management in stateful widgets. Calling setState within a stateful widget's methods notifies the framework that the widget's state has changed. This triggers a rebuild of the widget tree, starting from the changed widget and propagating upwards. The rebuilt widget tree reflects the latest state, updating the UI accordingly.

Maintaining State Consistency:

It's crucial to update state only within the widget's build methods or event handlers (like button press callbacks). Modifying state directly outside of these methods can lead to inconsistencies and unexpected behavior.

4.3 Provider State Management

While setState works well for simple scenarios, larger applications often require more sophisticated state management solutions. Provider is a popular third-party package that simplifies state management in Flutter.

ChangeNotifier and InheritedWidget:

Provider leverages two key concepts:

- **ChangeNotifier:** This is a mixin that provides functionality for notifying widgets that depend on its state whenever it changes.
- **InheritedWidget:** This is a base class for widgets that can share state information down the widget

tree.

Provider builds upon these concepts to create a centralized state management solution. You define a class extending ChangeNotifier to hold your application state. This state can then be accessed and consumed by widgets throughout the application using Provider.of and rebuild automatically when the state changes.

Code Example (Simplified):

```dart
class MyState extends ChangeNotifier {
  int count = 0;

  void increment() {
    count++;
```

Code Example (Simplified) (Continued):

```dart
    count++;
    notifyListeners(); // Notify listeners about state change
  }
```

```
}


class MyApp extends StatelessWidget {
  @override
  Widget build(BuildContext context) {
    return ChangeNotifierProvider<MyState>(
      create: (context) => MyState(),
      child: MaterialApp(
        home: MyHomePage(),
      ),
    );
  }
}


class MyHomePage extends StatelessWidget {
  @override
  Widget build(BuildContext context) {
    final state = Provider.of<MyState>(context); // Access
state using Provider.of
    return Scaffold(
      appBar: AppBar(
```

```
      title: Text('State Management'),
    ),
    body: Center(
      child: Column(
        mainAxisAlignment: MainAxisAlignment.center,
        children: [
          Text(
            'Count: ${state.count}',
            style: TextStyle(fontSize: 24.0),
          ),
          ElevatedButton(
            onPressed: () => state.increment(),
            child: Text('Increment'),
          ),
        ],
      ),
    ),
  );
  }
}
```

In this example, the MyState class manages the application state (count). The MyApp widget wraps the entire application tree with ChangeNotifierProvider, making the MyState instance accessible to any widget below it. The MyHomePage widget then retrieves the state using Provider.of and displays the count value. When the button is pressed, the increment method in MyState is called, updating the count and notifying listeners (widgets) through notifyListeners. This triggers a rebuild of MyHomePage with the updated count.

4.4 Advanced State Management Techniques

For complex applications with intricate state management needs, Flutter offers additional options:

- **BLoC (Business Logic Component):** This pattern separates business logic and data management from the UI. It involves events (user interactions or data changes) triggering state updates within the BLoC, which then notifies the UI through streams or sinks.
- **MobX:** This is a reactive state management library

that simplifies state management by automatically tracking dependencies and updating the UI whenever relevant state changes.

These techniques offer more granular control and scalability for state management in larger projects.

Choosing the Right Approach:

The choice of state management solution depends on your application's complexity. For simple scenarios, setState might be sufficient. As your app grows, consider using Provider for centralized state management, and for highly complex state interactions, explore BLoC or MobX.

By understanding stateful widgets and state management techniques, you'll be equipped to build dynamic and responsive UIs in your Flutter applications, ensuring that your UI reflects the current state of your app effectively.

This chapter has laid the foundation for building interactive and state-driven UIs in Flutter. The next chapters will delve deeper into more advanced topics like data handling, navigation, and integrating with external APIs.

CHAPTER 5

Working with Forms and User Input

User input forms are essential components of many applications. Flutter provides a robust set of widgets and techniques for building user-friendly and efficient forms. This chapter explores how to create forms, handle user input, and implement validation to ensure data integrity.

5.1 Text Fields and Form Management

- **TextField Widget:** The primary widget for capturing text input from users. It provides various customization options for styling, keyboard types (e.g., numeric, email), and input decoration.

```
TextField(
  decoration: InputDecoration(
    labelText: 'Username',
    border: OutlineInputBorder(),
  ),
```

)

- **Form Management:** While individual TextField
  widgets capture input, managing a collection of form
  fields often requires a higher-level structure. Flutter
  offers the Form widget for this purpose.

```
Form(
  child: Column(
    children: [
      TextField(
        decoration: InputDecoration(labelText: 'Email'),
      ),
      TextField(
        decoration: InputDecoration(labelText: 'Password'),
        obscureText: true, // Hide password characters
      ),
    ],
  ),
)
```

The Form widget provides a central location to manage the
state of all its child form fields. It also facilitates form

validation, which we'll explore next.

5.2 Form Validation with Form and TextFormField

- **Form Validation:** Ensuring user input adheres to specific criteria is crucial. Flutter allows you to validate form data before submission.

- **TextFormField:** A specialized form field widget that inherits from TextField and integrates with the Form widget for validation.

- **Validation Callbacks:** You can define validation rules using callbacks associated with the TextFormField properties:

  - validator: This function receives the user input as a string and returns an error message string if the input is invalid, or null if it's valid.

TextFormField(

decoration: InputDecoration(labelText: 'Email'),

```
validator: (value) {
  if (value == null || value.isEmpty) {
    return 'Please enter your email address.';
  }
                                                    if
(!RegExp(r"^[a-zA-Z0-9.a-z%+_]+@[a-z0-9.-]+\.[a-z]{2,}
$").hasMatch(value)) {
    return 'Please enter a valid email address.';
  }
  return null; // No error message, input is valid
},
)
```

When the form is submitted, the Form widget validates all its child TextFormField widgets using the provided validator functions. If any validation errors are found, an error message is displayed next to the corresponding field, guiding the user towards correcting their input.

5.3 Handling User Input Events

- **GestureDetector Widget:** Flutter provides the

GestureDetector widget for handling various user gestures like taps, swipes, and long presses on UI elements.

```
GestureDetector(
  onTap: () {
    print('Form submitted!');
    // Process form data here
  },
  child: Text('Submit'),
)
```

In this example, tapping the "Submit" text triggers the onTap callback, which can be used to perform actions like form submission and data processing.

- **Form Submission Events:** The Form widget also provides an onSaved callback that allows you to access the submitted form data after successful validation.

```
Form(
  onSaved: (values) {
    print(values['email']); // Access submitted email value
```

```
    print(values['password']);  // Access submitted
password value
    // Process form data here
  },
  child: /* Form fields... */,
)
```

By combining GestureDetector and Form events, you can capture user interactions and process submitted form data effectively.

5.4 Building Interactive and Dynamic Forms

- **Dynamic Forms:** In some scenarios, you might need forms that adapt based on user input. Flutter allows you to create dynamic forms by programmatically adding or removing form fields at runtime.

- **Form State Management:** For complex forms with intricate logic, consider using state management techniques like Provider or BLoC to manage the state of your form fields and dynamically update the UI based on user interactions.

By exploring these techniques, you can build forms that cater to diverse user input scenarios and ensure a smooth and interactive user experience within your Flutter applications.

CHAPTER 6

NAVIGATION AND ROUTING IN FLUTTER APPS

Navigation is a fundamental aspect of mobile applications, allowing users to move between different screens and views. Flutter provides a robust and flexible navigation system for building user-friendly and intuitive app experiences. This chapter explores various navigation concepts and techniques in Flutter.

6.1 Understanding Navigation Concepts

- **Navigation Patterns:** Flutter supports different navigation patterns to suit various app functionalities:

  - **Push:** This pattern adds a new screen (page) on top of the current screen, creating a forward navigation history. The user can navigate back to previous screens using a back button or gesture.

- ○ **Pop:** This pattern removes the current screen from the navigation stack, essentially navigating back to the previous screen.
- ○ **Replace:** This pattern replaces the current screen with a new screen, effectively clearing the navigation history up to that point.
- **Navigation Structure:** Planning your app's navigation structure beforehand is crucial. Consider the hierarchy of your screens and how users will navigate between them. Sketching out wireframes or user flows can be helpful in this process.

6.2 Using Navigator for Navigation

- **Navigator Widget:** The core navigation widget in Flutter is the Navigator. It manages the navigation stack, which is a LIFO (Last-In-First-Out) data structure that keeps track of the screens displayed in the app.

- **Pushing New Screens:** To navigate forward and push a new screen onto the stack, use Navigator.push(context, MaterialPageRoute(builder: (context) => NewScreen())). This pushes the NewScreen widget onto the navigation stack, displaying it on top of the current screen.

```
class HomeScreen extends StatelessWidget {
@override
Widget build(BuildContext context) {
 return Scaffold(
   appBar: AppBar(
    title: Text('Home'),
   ),
   body: Center(
    child: ElevatedButton(
     onPressed: () {
      Navigator.push(
       context,
          MaterialPageRoute(builder: (context) =>
```

```
DetailScreen()),
        );
      },
      child: Text('Go to Detail'),
    ),
   ),
  );
 }
}


class DetailScreen extends StatelessWidget {
 @override
 Widget build(BuildContext context) {
  return Scaffold(
   appBar: AppBar(
    title: Text('Detail'),
   ),
   body: Center(
    child: Text('Detail content'),
   ),
  );
```

```
    }
  }
}
```

In this example, pressing the button on the HomeScreen pushes the DetailScreen onto the navigation stack.

6.3 Navigation with Named Routes

- **Named Routes:** Defining named routes for your app's screens provides a more organized and readable approach to navigation. You can define routes in your main.dart file using the routes property of the MaterialApp widget.

```
routes: {
  '/home': (context) => HomeScreen(),
  '/detail': (context) => DetailScreen(),
},
```

- **Navigating with** Navigator.pushNamed(): Once you've defined named routes, you can use Navigator.pushNamed(context, '/detail') to navigate to the screen associated with the named route "/detail".

ElevatedButton(

onPressed: () => Navigator.pushNamed(context, '/detail'),

child: Text('Go to Detail'),

),

This approach promotes code reusability and clarity, as route definitions are centralized and navigation references the route names instead of widget types.

6.4 Passing Data Between Screens with Arguments

- **Sharing Data:** Often, you might need to share data between screens during navigation. Flutter allows you to pass arguments while pushing new screens.

- **Arguments with** Navigator.pushNamed(): When using named routes, you can add arguments as a map to the Navigator.pushNamed method call.

Navigator.pushNamed(context, '/detail', arguments: {'id': 123});

- **Receiving Arguments:** On the receiving screen, access the passed arguments using the ModalRoute.of(context).settings.arguments property.

```
class DetailScreen extends StatelessWidget {
@override
Widget build(BuildContext context) {
final id = ModalRoute.of(context).settings.arguments
as int;
// Use the received 'id' for data fetching or display
return Scaffold(
// ...
);
}
}
```

By employing these navigation techniques, you can create well-structured and user-friendly navigation flows within your Flutter applications.

CHAPTER 7

WORKING WITH APIS AND DATA FETCHING

This chapter builds upon the foundation laid in Chapter 5, diving deeper into making HTTP requests, handling asynchronous operations, and managing data retrieved from APIs.

7.1 Making HTTP Requests with HttpClient

The HttpClient class provides a low-level way to make HTTP requests and receive responses directly. It offers fine-grained control over headers, request body, and response handling.

- **Sending Requests:** You create an HttpClient instance and use its get, post, put, or delete methods depending on the desired HTTP verb for your API call.

```
final client = HttpClient();
final          request          =          await
client.getUrl(Uri.parse('https://api.example.com/data'));
final response = await request.close();
```

- **Handling Responses:** The response object contains the status code, headers, and a stream for the response body. You can process the response data based on the status code.

```
if (response.statusCode == 200) {
                final          data          =          await
response.transform(utf8.decoder).join();
  // Parse the data (JSON in this example)
} else {
  print('Error: ${response.statusCode}');
}
```

Note: Using HttpClient requires manual handling of lower-level details. For most scenarios, the http package (covered in Chapter 5) offers a simpler and more convenient approach.

7.2 Fetching Data with Async/Await

Asynchronous programming is essential for handling network calls that take time to complete. Flutter provides async and await keywords to manage asynchronous operations effectively.

- async **Functions:** Mark functions that perform asynchronous operations (like network calls) as async.

- await **Keyword:** Use await before a future-returning expression to pause execution of the current function until the future completes.

```
Future<String> fetchData() async {
        final response = await
http.get(Uri.parse('https://api.example.com/data'));
    if (response.statusCode == 200) {
```

```
return response.body;
} else {
throw Exception('Failed to load data');

}

}
```

In this example, the fetchData function is marked as async and uses await before the http.get call. The code pauses execution until the network call finishes, then processes the response.

7.3 Parsing JSON Data

- **JSON Format:** Many APIs return data in JSON (JavaScript Object Notation) format, a lightweight and human-readable data interchange format.

- **Parsing JSON:** Flutter doesn't have built-in JSON parsing functionality. Popular libraries like convert provide methods to decode JSON strings into Dart objects.

```
import 'package:convert/convert.dart';


Map<String, dynamic> parseJson(String jsonString) {
    return jsonDecode(jsonString) as Map<String,
dynamic>;
}
```

This function uses jsonDecode from the convert package to convert the JSON string into a Dart Map object. You can then access the parsed data using key-value lookups.

7.4 Caching and Offline Data Persistence

- **Caching:** Caching frequently accessed data locally on the device can improve performance and reduce network usage, especially for users with limited internet connectivity.

- **SharedPreferences:** A built-in Flutter mechanism for storing key-value pairs of data persistently on the device. It's suitable for simple data storage like user preferences or access tokens.

```
final prefs = await SharedPreferences.getInstance();
await prefs.setString('userData', jsonData); // Store JSON data
final storedData = prefs.getString('userData'); // Retrieve stored data
```

- **Hive:** A third-party package offering a more powerful and flexible solution for local data storage. It supports various data types and provides features like schema definition and encryption.

By employing these techniques, you can build robust networking functionality in your Flutter applications, efficiently handle asynchronous operations, and manage data retrieved from APIs effectively.

CHAPTER 8

WORKING WITH IMAGES AND MULTIMEDIA

This chapter delves into incorporating images, audio, and video elements into your Flutter applications. You'll explore techniques for displaying, optimizing, and manipulating multimedia content, along with integrating audio and video playback functionalities.

8.1 Displaying Images from Network and Assets

- **Loading Images:** Flutter provides various ways to load and display images:

  - **Network Images:** Use the Image.network constructor to load images from URLs.

Image.network('https://example.com/image.jpg')

Asset Images: Load images bundled within your app's

assets folder using the `AssetImage` constructor.

Image(image: AssetImage('assets/images/logo.png'))

- **FadeInImage:** To enhance user experience, consider using the FadeInImage widget. It displays a placeholder while the actual image loads, providing a smoother transition.

FadeInImage(

placeholder: AssetImage('assets/images/placeholder.png'),

image: NetworkImage('https://example.com/image.jpg'),

)

- **Optimizing Image Loading:** For a better user experience and efficient resource usage, consider techniques like:

  o **Caching Images:** Libraries like

cached_network_image can cache downloaded images locally, reducing network traffic for subsequent loads.

8.2 Advanced Image Features: Caching and Manipulation

- **Caching with** cached_network_image**:** This popular package simplifies network image loading and provides built-in caching functionality.

```
CachedNetworkImage(
  imageUrl: 'https://example.com/image.jpg',
    placeholder:       (context,      url)     =>
CircularProgressIndicator(),
  errorWidget: (context, url, error) => Icon(Icons.error),
)
```

- **Image Manipulation:** While Flutter doesn't have built-in image manipulation capabilities, third-party packages like image or flutter_image offer functionalities for resizing, cropping, and applying basic image filters.

```
import 'package:image/image.dart' as img;

Future<img.Image> resizeImage(String path, int width) async {
        final image = img.decodeImage(await File(path).readAsBytes());
    return img.resized(image, width: width);
  }
```

These techniques allow you to optimize image loading performance, customize image appearance, and cater to specific image manipulation needs in your app.

8.3 Playing Audio and Video

- **Audio Playback:** The audioplayers package provides functionalities for playing and managing audio files in your Flutter applications.

```
import 'package:audioplayers/audioplayers.dart';

final audioPlayer = AudioPlayer();

void playAudio(String url) async {
  await audioPlayer.play(url);
}

void stopAudio() async {
  await audioPlayer.stop();
}
```

- **Video Playback:** The video_player package empowers you to integrate video playback within your app.

```
import 'package:video_player/video_player.dart';
```

```dart
class VideoPlayerScreen extends StatefulWidget {
  @override
  _VideoPlayerScreenState createState() =>
_VideoPlayerScreenState();
}

class _VideoPlayerScreenState extends
State<VideoPlayerScreen> {
  VideoPlayerController _controller;

  @override
  void initState() {
   super.initState();
   _controller = VideoPlayerController.network(
     'https://www.example.com/video.mp4',
   );
   _controller.initialize().then((_) => setState(() {}));
  }

  @override
  void dispose() {
```

```
_controller.dispose();
super.dispose();
}


@override
Widget build(BuildContext context) {
  return VideoPlayer(_controller);
}
}
```

These packages offer functionalities like playback control, seeking, and volume adjustments, enabling you to incorporate audio and video playback features into your app.

8.4 Building Interactive Multimedia Experiences

- **Interactive Audio and Video:** Combine user interaction with audio and video playback to create engaging experiences. You can use buttons or gestures to control playback (play, pause, seek) or adjust volume.

```
FloatingActionButton(
 onPressed: () {
  if (_controller.value.isPlaying) {
   _controller.pause();
  } else {
   _controller.play();
  }
 },
  child: Icon(_controller.value.isPlaying ? Icons.pause :
Icons.play_arrow),
 )
```

By integrating these functionalities, you can create dynamic and user-controlled multimedia experiences within your Flutter

- **Interactive Multimedia Experiences :** In addition to basic playback control, you can explore more advanced features:

  o **Background Audio:** Utilize background audio playback to enable audio playback even when the app is minimized or in the background. Consider platform-specific limitations and user preferences for background audio usage.

o **Customizable Controls:** Develop custom user interfaces for controlling audio and video playback, tailoring the experience to your app's design and functionality.

o **Integration with Other Features:** Combine multimedia elements with other app functionalities. For example, playing background music during a game or displaying product videos within an e-commerce app.

By incorporating user interaction and exploring these advanced features, you can create engaging and interactive multimedia experiences within your Flutter applications.

8.5 Building Custom Widgets

While Flutter provides a rich set of built-in widgets, there will be times when you need to create custom widgets to meet your specific UI requirements. This chapter provides a basic understanding of building custom widgets in Flutter.

- **Custom Widget Class:** Define a new Dart class that extends the StatelessWidget or StatefulWidget base class depending on whether your widget needs to manage internal state.

```
class CustomButton extends StatelessWidget {
  final String text;
  final VoidCallback onPressed;

  const CustomButton({required this.text, required this.onPressed});

  @override
  Widget build(BuildContext context) {
    return ElevatedButton(
      onPressed: onPressed,
```

```
    child: Text(text),
   );
 }
}
```

- **Building the UI:** Implement the build method to define the UI structure of your custom widget using other Flutter widgets.

- **Custom Widget Properties:** You can define constructor arguments or properties to allow customization of your custom widget's behavior and appearance.

- **Reusability:** Custom widgets promote code reusability by encapsulating specific UI components and functionalities. You can use your custom widget throughout your app or even share it as a reusable package.

By understanding these principles, you can create custom widgets that extend Flutter's built-in widget library and cater to the unique UI requirements of your application.

8.6 Testing Your Flutter Apps

- **Importance of Testing:** Robust testing practices are crucial for ensuring the quality, stability, and reliability of your Flutter applications. Testing helps identify bugs and regressions early in the development process.

- **Testing Tools:** Flutter offers various testing tools and frameworks:

  - **Widget Tests:** Test the UI and behavior of individual widgets using the flutter test command and the widget_tester package.
  - **Unit Tests:** Test isolated units of code (functions, classes) to ensure their correctness. Popular frameworks like test and mockito are

commonly used.

- ○ **Integration Tests:** Test how different parts of your app interact with each other.

By employing these testing strategies, you can write well-tested and reliable Flutter applications, contributing to a smoother development experience and a more stable app for your users.

This chapter has equipped you with the knowledge to incorporate multimedia elements, build custom widgets, and implement basic testing practices in your Flutter applications.

CHAPTER 9

ANIMATIONS AND VISUAL EFFECTS IN FLUTTER

Animations play a vital role in creating engaging and user-friendly interfaces. Flutter provides robust animation capabilities, allowing you to bring your app's UI to life with smooth and visually appealing transitions. This chapter explores different animation techniques and tools for building dynamic and interactive experiences in your Flutter apps.

9.1 Understanding Animations in Flutter

- **Animation Techniques:** Flutter offers two primary animation approaches:

  - **Tween Animations:** These animations smoothly transition between two states (values) over a specified duration. You define the starting and ending values for properties like opacity, size, or color, and Flutter handles the interpolation between them.

○ **Implicit Animations:** Certain Flutter widgets (like AnimatedContainer, AnimatedOpacity) provide built-in implicit animations for specific property changes. These animations offer a simpler way to animate basic widget properties without requiring manual tween animation setup.

By understanding these techniques, you can choose the most appropriate approach for your animation needs.

9.2 Creating Animations with AnimatedBuilder

• **AnimatedBuilder:** This widget is ideal for simple animations where a property value changes over time. It rebuilds its child widget whenever the animation value updates, allowing you to dynamically adjust the widget's appearance.

```
class AnimatedOpacityExample extends StatefulWidget
{

  @override
    _AnimatedOpacityExampleState createState() =>
_AnimatedOpacityExampleState();

  }


  class    _AnimatedOpacityExampleState    extends
State<AnimatedOpacityExampleState> {
  bool _visible = true;

  void toggleVisibility() {
    setState(() {
    _visible = !_visible;
    });
  }


  @override
  Widget build(BuildContext context) {
    return Column(
      children: [
```

```
AnimatedOpacity(
  opacity: _visible ? 1.0 : 0.0,
  duration: Duration(seconds: 1),
  child: Text(
    'This text fades in and out.',
    style: TextStyle(fontSize: 24.0),
  ),
),
ElevatedButton(
  onPressed: toggleVisibility,
  child: Text('Toggle Visibility'),
),
],
);
}
}
```

In this example, the AnimatedOpacity widget animates the opacity of the Text widget based on the _visible state. The AnimatedBuilder rebuilds itself whenever _visible changes, updating the text's opacity accordingly.

9.3 Advanced Animations with AnimationController

- **AnimationController:** For complex animations with fine-grained control over timing, curves, and behavior, use the AnimationController class. It provides granular control over the animation timeline and allows you to define custom animation sequences.

```
class AnimatedLogo extends StatefulWidget {
@override
        _AnimatedLogoState    createState()    =>
_AnimatedLogoState();
  }


  class          _AnimatedLogoState          extends
State<AnimatedLogo> {
  AnimationController _controller;
  Animation<double> _animation;


  @override
```

```
void initState() {
  super.initState();
    _controller = AnimationController(vsync: this,
duration: Duration(seconds: 2));
    _animation = Tween<double>(begin: 0.0, end:
360.0).animate(_controller);
}

@override
void dispose() {
  _controller.dispose();
  super.dispose();
}

@override
Widget build(BuildContext context) {
  return Transform.rotate(
    angle: _animation,
    child: FlutterLogo(size: 100.0),
  );
}
```

}

Here, the AnimationController manages the animation timeline. The Tween defines the animation's starting and ending values (rotation angle in this case). The Transform.rotate widget applies the animation value to the FlutterLogo, resulting in a rotating logo animation.

9.4 Exploring Third-Party Animation Packages

- **Pre-built Animations:** Several third-party packages offer pre-built animations that you can easily integrate into your app.

  - **Rive:** A powerful animation tool that allows you to create complex, interactive animations using state machines and user input.

  - **flutter_spinkit:** Provides a collection of predefined loading spinners and progress indicators, saving you time and effort in creating basic animations.

- **Lottie Animations:** Lottie animations are lightweight JSON-based animations that can be easily integrated into Flutter apps using the flutter_lottie package. They offer rich and interactive animation possibilities.

By incorporating these advanced animation techniques and third-party packages, you can create dynamic and engaging animations that enhance the user experience of your Flutter applications.

This chapter has equipped you with the foundation for creating animations in Flutter. By understanding different animation techniques and utilizing tools like AnimatedBuilder and AnimationController, you can build smooth and visually appealing animations for your app's UI.

9.5 Building Custom Animations with StaggeredAnimations

- **StaggeredAnimations:** The flutter_staggered_animations package simplifies the creation of staggered animations, where multiple elements animate with a slight delay or offset from each other. This can create a cascading or wave-like effect, adding visual interest to your app.

```
import
'package:flutter_staggered_animations/flutter_staggered_a
nimations.dart';


class StaggeredList extends StatelessWidget {

  final List<String> items;


  const StaggeredList({required this.items});


  @override
```

```
Widget build(BuildContext context) {

return StaggeredGridView.countBuilder(

crossAxisCount: 2,

itemCount: items.length,

itemBuilder: (context, index) =>
StaggeredGridItem.count(

crossAxisCount: 2,

mainAxisSpacing: 4.0,

crossAxisSpacing: 4.0,

child: Container(

color: Colors.grey[300],

child: Center(child: Text(items[index])),

),

animation: AnimatedStaggeredFadeIn(
```

```
      duration: Duration(milliseconds: 500),

          delay: Duration(milliseconds: index * 100), //
Staggered delay

      ),

      ),

                staggeredTileBuilder:    (index)    =>
StaggeredTile.count(2, 1),

    );

  }

}
```

In this example, the StaggeredGridView.countBuilder creates a grid of items. Each item is wrapped with StaggeredGridItem.count and uses AnimatedStaggeredFadeIn animation. This animation provides a fading-in effect for each item with a slight delay based on its index, creating a staggered entrance animation for the list.

9.6 Animation Performance Considerations

- **Performance Optimization:** While animations can enhance user experience, it's crucial to optimize their performance to avoid jank or slowdowns. Here are some tips:

    - **Minimize Unnecessary Rebuilds:** Use techniques like setState selectively to avoid unnecessary UI rebuilds that can trigger re-animations.
    - **Utilize Efficient Animation Classes:** Prefer AnimationController for complex animations, but consider AnimatedBuilder or implicit animations for simpler cases, as they can be more performant.
    - **Profile and Optimize:** Use Flutter's profiling tools to identify performance bottlenecks in

your animations and optimize them accordingly.

By following these practices, you can ensure your animations enhance the user experience without compromising app performance.

Animations can transform a static app into a dynamic and engaging experience. By effectively utilizing the techniques and tools covered in this chapter, you can add life to your Flutter app's UI and create a more captivating and user-friendly experience for your audience.

CHAPTER 10

DEPLOYING YOUR FLUTTER APP

Congratulations! You've built a fantastic Flutter app and are ready to share it with the world. This chapter guides you through the process of preparing your app for release, deploying it to app stores, and managing its lifecycle after launch.

10.1 Building Your App for Release

Before deploying your app, you need to configure it for release mode. This involves generating platform-specific builds optimized for app store submission.

- **Configuring Build Settings:**

  - **Android:**

    - Update your build.gradle file to configure signing keys and release settings. You'll need to create a keystore containing your signing credentials.

■ Enable ProGuard/R8 for code shrinking and optimization.

○

○ **iOS:**

■ Configure your Xcode project for App Store distribution. This includes creating a signing certificate and provisioning profile.

■ Ensure your app adheres to Apple's App Store guidelines (refer to https://developer.apple.com/app-store/review/guidelines/).

Understanding App Signing and Certificates:

• **Signing Keys:** A cryptographic key pair used to sign your app before submitting it to the app store. Signing ensures the app originates from you and hasn't been tampered with.

- **Certificates:** Digital certificates associated with your signing key pair. These certificates verify your identity as a trusted developer.

Obtaining Signing Credentials:

- **Android:** Generate a keystore using the keytool command-line tool.
- **iOS:** Generate signing certificates and provisioning profiles within the Apple Developer Portal (https://developer.apple.com/programs/).

Security Considerations:

- Keep your signing credentials secure. Sharing them can compromise your app's integrity.
- Consider using a secure keystore management solution.

10.2 Deploying to App Stores (Google Play, App Store)

- **Creating App Store Accounts and Listings:**

- **Google Play:** Create a Google Play Developer account and configure your app's listing details like title, description, screenshots, and category.
- **App Store:** Enroll in the Apple Developer Program and create an App Store Connect account. Set up your app's listing information following Apple's guidelines.

•

- **Following App Store Submission Process:**

  - Both app stores have specific submission processes. Ensure your app meets their technical requirements, content guidelines, and review criteria.
  - Provide clear instructions, screenshots, and videos showcasing your app's functionality during submission.
  - Be prepared to address any feedback or issues raised during the app review process.

Tips for a Smooth Submission:

- Start planning your app store submission early in development.
- Test your app thoroughly on real devices before submission.
- Familiarize yourself with each app store's guidelines and review process.

10.3 Distributing Your App Through Other Channels

While app stores are the primary distribution channels, you can explore alternatives:

- **Beta Testing Platforms:** Services like Firebase Test Lab or Beta by Google Play allow you to distribute pre-release versions of your app to a limited audience for testing and feedback.
- **Direct Distribution:** Share your app's APK or IPA file with testers or early adopters through private channels.

Considerations for Alternative Distribution:

- **Security:** Be cautious when sharing app builds outside app stores. Implement measures to prevent unauthorized distribution.
- **Updates:** Manually updating apps distributed outside app stores can be cumbersome.

10.4 Maintaining and Updating Your App

- **Implementing Version Control (Git):**

  - Use a version control system like Git to track changes in your app's codebase.
  - Git allows you to collaborate with other developers, revert to previous versions if needed, and manage code releases effectively.
  - Popular Git hosting platforms like GitHub offer additional features for managing your project.

- **Pushing Updates to App Stores and Handling Bug Fixes:**

- Once you've fixed bugs or implemented new features, create a new release and update your app store listings.

- Provide clear release notes outlining changes and improvements in each update.

- Address user feedback and bug reports promptly to maintain a positive app reputation.

Additional Considerations:

- **App Analytics:** Integrate app analytics tools to track user behavior and app performance. Use this data to identify areas for improvement and make data-driven decisions for future updates.

- **Crashlytics:** Utilize crash reporting tools like Firebase Crashlytics to identify and fix crashes that occur in the real world.

- **Community Engagement:** Actively engage with your user base. Respond to reviews, answer questions, and provide support to build a loyal community around your app.

By following these guidelines and best practices, you can successfully deploy your Flutter app, manage its lifecycle effectively, and keep your users engaged with ongoing updates and improvements.

ABOUT THE AUTHOR

Writer's Bio:

 Benjamin Evans, a respected figure in the tech world, is known for his insightful commentary and analysis. With a strong educational background likely in fields such as computer science, engineering, or business, he brings a depth of knowledge to his discussions on emerging technologies and industry trends. Evans' knack for simplifying complex concepts, coupled with his innate curiosity and passion for innovation, has established him as a go-to source for understanding the dynamics of the digital landscape. Through articles, speeches, and social media, he shares his expertise and offers valuable insights into the impact of technology on society.